INTRODUCING DINOSAURS

MAIASAURA

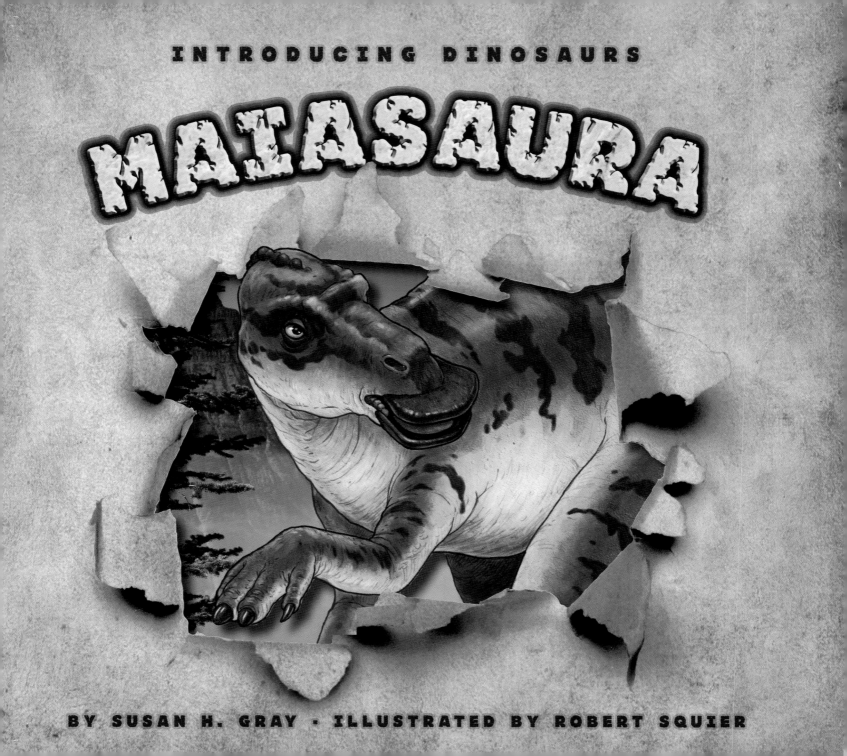

BY SUSAN H. GRAY · ILLUSTRATED BY ROBERT SQUIER

The Child's World

Published by The Child's World®
1980 Lookout Drive • Mankato, MN 56003-1705
800-599-READ • www.childsworld.com

ACKNOWLEDGMENTS
The Child's World®: Mary Berendes, Publishing Director
The Design Lab: Kathleen Petelinsek, Art Direction and Design;
Victoria Stanley and Anna Petelinsek, Page Production
Editorial Directions: E. Russell Primm, Editor; Lucia Raatma, Copy Editor;
Dina Rubin, Proofreader; Tim Griffin, Indexer

PHOTO CREDITS
©stevegeer/iStock: cover, 2–3; ©Getty Images/Time Life Pictures: 4;
©Layne Kennedy/Corbis: 8 (left); ©William Manning/Corbis: 8–9;
©Kamchatka/Dreamstime.com: 14–15; ©Danny Lehman/Corbis: 16 (top);
©Granitepeaker/Dreamstime.com: 16–17

LIBRARY OF CONGRESS CATALOGING-IN-PUBLICATION DATA
Gray, Susan Heinrichs.
  Maiasaura / by Susan H. Gray; illustrated by Robert Squier.
    p. cm.—(Introducing dinosaurs)
  Includes bibliographical references and index.
  ISBN 978-1-60253-239-7 (lib. bound: alk. paper)
  1. Maiasaura—Juvenile literature. I. Squier, Robert, ill. II. Title.
  QE862.O65G74562 2009
  567.914—dc22   2009001626

Printed in the United States of America
Mankato, Minnesota
May, 2010
PA02063

TABLE OF CONTENTS

WHAT WAS MAIASAURA?

Maiasaura (my-uh-SAWR-ah) was a dinosaur that lived long ago. Its name means "good mother **lizard**." *Maiasaura* left many **fossils** behind. **Scientists** have found its bones and teeth. They have found its eggs and nests. They have even found fossils of its babies!

Jack Horner (right) gave Maiasaura its name. He also found the first fossilized Maiasaura eggs. Maiasaura mothers paid close attention to their babies. They fed them and protected them from other dinosaurs.

WHAT DID *MAIASAURA* LOOK LIKE?

Maiasaura was big. It weighed about the same as two cars. It had a big belly and a long, heavy tail. It **lumbered** along on four enormous legs. Sometimes, it rose up and ran on two legs.

Maiasaura was very large. It would cause a traffic jam if one walked through the streets today!

Maiasaura had a wide, flat head. It had a hard beak instead of lips. There were no teeth in the front of its mouth. But there were hundreds of teeth along the sides of its mouth!

Scientists often discuss the fossils they find and share information with each other (above). Scientists learned much about Maiasaura by digging up its fossilized bones. This jawbone fossil (right) shows the many rows of teeth that Maiasaura had.

WHAT WAS A *MAIASAURA* NEST LIKE?

Maiasaura built its nest on the ground. It was a **shallow** pit with a rim of mud. The mother dinosaur laid about twenty-five eggs in the pit. She covered them with dirt, moss, and leaves. That kept the eggs warm.

Soon, the eggs hatched. The babies were weak and helpless. As they grew, they stayed close to their families.

Maiasaura *made its nest carefully. This is one reason why it was called "good mother lizard."*

HOW DID MAIASAURA SPEND ITS LIFE?

Maiasaura spent its whole life with its herd. The **herd** of dinosaurs traveled together. They searched for food and water together. They stayed together as they built their nests. They raised their babies together.

Maiasaura *herds were like big families. It was difficult for other dinosaurs to attack them because of this.*

14

Maiasaura was not a fierce hunter. It did not eat other dinosaurs. It just ate plants. Other dinosaurs could easily attack it. But *Maiasaura* was safe in its herd. There, many *Maiasaura* could watch for danger all at once.

Plants such as this fern would have made a tasty meal for Maiasaura. Maiasaura did not have the right teeth to eat meat.

HOW DO WE KNOW ABOUT *MAIASAURA?*

Maiasaura fossils tell us about its life. Scientists have found the fossils of *Maiasaura* herds. Some herds were made up of thousands of *Maiasaura!*

Fossils of Maiasaura footprints (above) can tell scientists a number of things. They can learn how fast Maiasaura moved and where it lived. Scientists search for fossils all around the world, including the mountains of Montana (right).

17

Fossils in *Maiasaura* nesting places tell us even more. Their eggs were the size of grapefruits. Each **newborn** was as long as a loaf of bread. The nest's rim kept the babies from crawling away. *Maiasaura* could easily watch over her young. *Maiasaura* really was a good mother!

Hungry Maiasaura *babies waited in the nest for their mother to bring food. The nest was important for the safety of the young* Maiasaura.

WHERE HAVE MAIASAURA BONES BEEN FOUND?

Canada

Montana

NORTH AMERICA

EUROPE

ASIA

Atlantic Ocean

Pacific Ocean

AFRICA

SOUTH AMERICA

Indian Ocean

AUSTRALIA

Map Key

Where *Maiasaura* bones have been found

Where possible *Maiasaura* fossils or tracks have been found

Southern Ocean

WHO FINDS THE BONES?

Fossil hunters find dinosaur bones. Some fossil hunters are scientists. Others are people who hunt fossils for fun. They go to areas where dinosaurs once lived. They find bones in rocky places, in mountainsides, and in deserts.

When fossil hunters discover dinosaur bones, they get busy. They use picks to chip rocks away from the fossils. They use small brushes to sweep off any dirt. They take pictures of the fossils. They also write notes about where the fossils were found. They want to remember everything!

Fossil hunters use many tools to dig up fossils. It is very important to use the right tools so the fossils do not get damaged.

GLOSSARY

fossils (*FOSS-ullz*) Fossils are preserved parts of plants and animals that died long ago.

herd (*HURD*) A herd is a group of animals that travel together.

lizard (*LIZ-urd*) A lizard is a scaly animal that walks on four legs.

lumbered (*LUM-burd*) An animal that lumbered along is one that walked slowly and heavily.

Maiasaura (*my-uh-SAWR-ah*) *Maiasaura* was a dinosaur that lived about 80 million years ago.

newborn (*NOO-born*) A newborn is an animal that has just been born.

scientists (*SY-un-tists*) Scientists are people who study how things work through observations and experiments.

shallow (*SHAL-oh*) Something that is shallow is not deep.

BOOKS

Gray, Susan. *Maiasaura.*
Mankato, MN: Child's World, 2004.

Parker, Steve. *Dinosaurus: The Complete Guide to Dinosaurs.*
New York: Firefly Books, 2003.

Searl, Duncan. *The Maiasaura Nests: Jack Horner's Dinosaur Eggs.*
New York: Bearport Publishing, 2006.

Zoehfeld, Kathleen. *Dinosaur Babies.*
New York: HarperTrophy, 1999.

WEB SITES

Visit our Web site for lots of links about *Maiasaura:*

CHILDSWORLD.COM/LINKS

*Note to Parents, Teachers, and Librarians: We routinely verify our Web links to make
sure they are safe, active sites—so encourage your readers to check them out!*

INDEX

ABOUT THE AUTHOR

Susan Gray has written more than ninety books for children. She especially likes to write about animals. Susan lives in Cabot, Arkansas, with her husband, Michael, and many pets.

ABOUT THE ILLUSTRATOR

Robert Squier has been drawing dinosaurs ever since he could hold a crayon. Today, instead of using crayons, he uses pencils, paint, and the computer. Robert lives in New Hampshire with his wife, Jessica, and a house full of dinosaur toys. *Stegosaurus* is his favorite dinosaur.